Oprah Winfrey

The Life, Lessons & Rules for Success

Influential Individuals

Chapter One: Early Life

(handwritten annotation in margin: No, I will not let you treat me this way)

---

*"To have the kind of internal strength
and internal courage it takes to say,
'No, I will not let you treat me this way',
is what success is all about." – Oprah
Winfrey*

Orpah Gail Winfrey was born on January 29, 1954 in
Kosciusko, Mississippi to Vernita Lee, an unwed teenage
housemaid. The name 'Orpah' was taken from a character in
the Biblical book of Ruth, and is the name listed on her birth
certificate. Growing up, however, people mispronounced
Orpah's name frequently to "Oprah", and soon she became
more widely known by this name. The exact identity of
Oprah's biological father has been the subject of some
controversy, usually attributed to Vernon Winfrey, who
worked as a coal miner and barber and eventually became a

city councilman. Vernon is said to have had a brief relationship with Oprah's mother which ended after her conception. Another person, World War II veteran and Mississippi farmer Noah Robinson, Sr., has also claimed to be the biological father of Oprah.

After Oprah was born, her mother moved to the northern region of Mississippi to live with Oprah's grandmother, Hattie Mae Lee. Growing up with her grandmother in rural Mississippi, Oprah's childhood was one of intense poverty. The young Winfrey often had to wear hessian overalls, made out of potato sacks, and this earned her the moniker "Sack Girl". While other children had toys and pets, Oprah had pet cockroaches and a doll she carved from a corn cob.

Despite the adverse situation, Oprah showed brilliance as a child. Her grandmother, Hattie Mae, taught her how to read by the age of three and would take the young Oprah with her to church. Oprah soon became known as "The Preacher" because of her ability to recite entire Bible verses at a time. Oprah's grandmother was quite a strict disciplinarian, using corporal punishment when the child did not perform her assigned chores or if she misbehaved.

"I grew up in an environment where children were seen and not heard," Oprah once told David Letterman at a lecture series held at Indiana's Ball State University. "I was beaten regularly ... I went to a well to get some water and carry it in a bucket. And I was playing in the water with my fingers, and my grandmother had seen me out the window and she didn't like it. She whipped me so badly that I had welts on my back and the welts would bleed."

When Winfrey was six years old, she moved back in with her mother who was now working as a maid in Milwaukee, Wisconsin. From the rural farming community in Mississippi, Winfrey was uprooted to an inner-city neighborhood with little attention and care from her mother, who was working very long hours. Oprah's mother, Vernita Lee, soon had another daughter, Patricia, and found it difficult to raise the pair of them. It was then decided that Oprah would live temporarily with Vernon Winfrey, purported to be her biological father. Vernon was residing in Nashville, Tennessee. It would be the first time that Oprah would experience having her own bed and bedroom. She was enrolled in Wharton Elementary School and showed her skills in public speaking at school and church events. This arrangement did not last very long, and Oprah was soon living with her mother again who by this time had given birth to a son named Jeffrey.

Things took a turn for the worse around this time for Oprah. At the age of nine, she became a victim of rape and sexual

—

molestation by a cousin, uncle, and another friend of the family. She revealed the harrowing details of this experience in her own talk show years later, stating that she was first raped by a 19-year-old cousin who was babysitting her and her siblings. After the first incident, the cousin bought her ice cream, blood still streaming down her leg, and forbade her from telling anyone about the abuse. Over the next few years, Oprah would be repeatedly molested by the three men. Despite what was going on privately, Oprah still managed to develop a love for reading, and this was noticed by one of her teachers at Milwaukee's Lincoln Middle School, Gene Abrams. Abrams assisted in transferring Oprah to Nicolet High School, an all-white school in nearby Glendale. In other areas of the country, this would have been a difficult transition, but according to Oprah, it was easy for her to get used to the new school. "In 1968 it was real hip to know a black person, so I was very popular," she recalls.

Throughout those years, the sexual abuse at the hands of her cousin, uncle, and 'family friend' continued, but Oprah could not talk about the ordeal with her mother, who was still very busy with work and provided very little guidance. Oprah soon started acting out, becoming involved in several instances of stealing, cutting classes, and running away from home. At the age of 14, Oprah found out that she was

—

7

pregnant, but the baby boy was born prematurely and died soon after. After several more instances of delinquent behavior and being turned away from a teenage girls' detention home, Oprah's mother decided that she should live with her father again in Tennessee.

Vernon was also quite a disciplinarian, but provided the encouragement and guidance that teenage Oprah needed. Vernon would require Oprah to read one book each week and then write a report about it. Soon, Oprah's grades improved and her errant ways as a teenager became less frequent. She became an honor student, even being selected as one of two Tennessee students to attend the White House Conference on Youth held in Colorado.

Oprah credits the change in her life direction to a book she read as a 16-year-old, the Maya Angelou autobiography, "I Know Why The Caged Bird Sings". Oprah's outlook on life, which had been quite difficult until that point, completely changed after she read the autobiography. "I read it over and over, I had never before read a book that validated my own existence," she once stated.

With a renewed purpose in life, Oprah decided to get her life back on the right track, focusing on achieving a good education and developing her skills in public speaking. In 1970, she won a public speaking contest at a local Elks' Club, and was awarded a four-year college scholarship. More opportunities arose, including an interview with Nashville's WVOL radio station which led to her representing the station at the city's Miss Fire Prevention beauty contest. Oprah became the very first African-American to win the competition.

It was this experience with WVOL that would become Oprah's first experience in journalism, a precursor to the hugely successful broadcasting career she would soon be able to achieve. Oprah accepted a part-time job as a news presenter at the radio station, graduated from high school at the age of 17, and set out to conquer the world.

Chapter Summary

- Oprah was born in Kosciusko, Mississippi on January 29, 1954.
- Her real name is Orpah Gail Winfrey. She was named after a Biblical figure from the Book of Ruth, but her name was often mispronounced, and Oprah became her more popular nickname.
- Oprah's mother, Vernita Lee, was an unwed teenage housemaid.
- Vernon Winfrey is often referred to as her biological father, but another man, Noah Robinson, Sr., has also claimed to be Oprah's biological father.
- Oprah grew up in abject poverty in rural Mississippi with her grandmother, Hattie Mae, where she often had to wear clothes made from potato sacks.
- The young Oprah showed talent in public speaking, reciting Bible verses at church and earning the nickname "The Preacher".
- Oprah was sexually abused by several family members starting at the age of nine. She became pregnant at 13, gave birth prematurely, and the baby boy died within two weeks.
- Vernon Winfrey provided the guidance that the teenaged Oprah did not get from her mother, and a turnaround in her high school years opened several doors of opportunity for Oprah, including a part-time news reading position at a Nashville radio station and a four-year college scholarship.

Chapter Two: College Years & Breaking into Television

> *"I know what it feels like to not be wanted ... you can use it as a stepping stone to build great empathy for people." - Oprah Winfrey*

Oprah Winfrey graduated from senior high school at the young age of 17. She decided to enroll at Tennessee State University and major in Speech Communications and Performing Arts. While in college, Oprah had already caught the eye of a local CBS television station and was offered a job as a co-anchor. Oprah was hesitant to accept the offer. At the time, she was still juggling college and her job as news presenter at WVOL. Eventually her speech professor convinced her that the job could help launch her broadcast career.

Her professor was able to convince Oprah to take the job offer by reminding her that the reason people go to college was to get job offers from TV networks such as CBS. Oprah became the first female African-American news anchor for Nashville's WLAC-TV station, and their youngest news anchor at the time. At just nineteen years old and just a sophomore in college, Oprah was already getting prime training and exposure in the world of broadcast television.

Soon, Oprah wanted to try and find work outside of the Nashville market, and got a job offer from WJZ-TV in Baltimore, Maryland to co-anchor their 6pm newscast. The job offer was given just a few months before Oprah's college graduation, and she had to make a choice whether to finish college and get her degree, or move to Baltimore and accept the TV job. She eventually chose Baltimore, and joined WJZ-TV in 1976.

Oprah's stint as co-anchor in WJZ-TV's evening newscast did not go as well as planned, and she was soon removed from the position. She did, however, stay with WJZ-TV and worked several other jobs for the station until being given the Baltimore edition of the "Dialing for Dollars" segment, and a local talk show called *People Are Talking*. This would be Oprah's first foray into TV talk show hosting, and she immediately took a liking to it. She stayed in this talk show for seven years, honing her hosting skills.

In 1983, Oprah made another move, this time to Chicago, Illinois. There she would host a 30-minute morning talk show airing on WLS-TV, *AM Chicago*. Before being offered the job, Oprah had sent WLS-TV several recorded tapes of her Baltimore talk show. At the time, AM Chicago was suffering from very low ratings - a challenge for Oprah.

She recalls, "My first day in Chicago, September 4, 1983. I set foot in this city, and just walking down the street, it was like roots, like the motherland. I knew I belonged here."

Oprah's style as a talk show host proved to be a hit among Chicago viewers. Within just a few months after taking over the hosting duties for *AM Chicago*, the show overtook then ratings-leader *Donahue*, becoming the highest-rated TV talk show in the Chicago market. Popular film critic Roger Ebert took notice of Oprah and her rising popularity, and recognized this as something potentially special and ready for a much bigger audience.

It all started when Ebert, along with his friend Gene Siskel, guested on Oprah's previous talk show in Baltimore. Ebert noticed what a natural Oprah was as a talk show host, and their paths crossed once again when Oprah got the *AM Chicago* gig and Ebert was a guest host. He convinced Oprah to accept a syndication offer being tendered by King World, a major TV production and syndication company which later was incorporated into CBS Television Distribution. King World rose to prominence as the distributor of *Our Gang* shorts, which were later renamed *The Little Rascals*. King World also held the syndication rights to *Wheel of Fortune, The Merv Griffin Show*, and *Jeopardy!*

As ratings rose, Oprah changed the name of the morning talk show to *The Oprah Winfrey Show*, and soon the show was being syndicated across the United States. From a half-hour show, the nationally-syndicated program expanded to a full hour, with Oprah also becoming the producer through her own company, Harpo Productions. In syndication, *The Oprah Winfrey Show* again went head-to-head versus *Donahue* and prevailed in the ratings, with almost twice the amount of her competitor. Harpo Productions took over complete ownership and production of *The Oprah Winfrey Show* by 1988, acquiring the program from Capitol Cities and ABC, and building a brand-new 100,000-square-foot production studio in Chicago, worth over $20 million.

Oprah had struck gold, and viewers resonated with her hosting style and the topics she presented on her daytime talk show. Soon, the fast-rising television star would venture into other media platforms all while maintaining a solid foothold in the daytime TV ratings segment.

Chapter Summary

- After graduating from high school at 17 years old, Oprah Winfrey enrolled at Tennessee State University to take up Speech Communications and Performing Arts.
- During her first two years in college, Oprah still managed to juggle her studies and her job as a news presenter at Nashville's WVOL radio station.
- Nashville station WLAC-TV, a CBS affiliate, offered a co-anchor position to Oprah which she initially turned down. Later encouraged by a speech professor, she accepted the job.
- Before graduating from college, Oprah was offered a co-anchor position at Baltimore's WJZ-TV which she accepted. She lasted in the position about a year.
- Oprah was then moved to other assignments, including "Dialing for Dollars" and the talk show *People Are Talking*.
- After seven years of hosting *People Are Talking*, Oprah moved to Chicago and took over as host of the talk show AM Chicago. In just a few months, AM Chicago moved from the bottom of the ratings game to Chicago's top-rated talk show, beating Donahue.
- Soon, AM Chicago was renamed The Oprah Winfrey Show, and started national syndication with King World. Nationally, The Oprah Winfrey Show would also go on to overtake erstwhile ratings leader Donahue.

Chapter Three: The Queen of All Media Emerges

"I want to let people see the light inside themselves." - Oprah Winfrey

---

Oprah Winfrey is often called the "Queen of all Media" because of her seemingly inescapable presence in modern mass media, whether it is television, publications, online platforms, or other broadcast and print ventures. Her encompassing presence in the world of entertainment and broadcasting across different platforms can be traced back to her first stints as a radio news presenter and TV anchor. It is worth noting that her forays into film introduced a broader audience to her rising popularity.

Oprah's debut as a film actress was in the 1985 period drama *The Color Purple*, based on the novel by Alice Walker. The novel, a Pulitzer Prize winner, tackled many problems that African American women had to face in the early 20th century, such as poverty, domestic violence, racism, sexism, incest, pedophilia, and civil rights. The story is set in a rural area of Georgia and revolves around the character of Celie, who along with other African American women of her time must overcome the misogyny, inequality, and racism.

The film adaptation of *The Color Purple* was directed by Steven Spielberg and adapted for film by Menno Meyjes. It was a far cry from the blockbusters that had made Spielberg a household name, and featured Danny Glover, Desreta Jackson, Margaret Avery, Adolph Caesar, and Rae Dawn Chong. Playing the role of the central character Celie Harris-Johnson was Whoopi Goldberg, also in her very first film role. Before *The Color Purple*, Oprah's only experience in acting was in a one-woman show, *The History of Black Women Through Drama and Song*, performed in a 1978 theater festival for African Americans.

Oprah has candidly recounted in many interviews that *The Color Purple* was already one of her favorite books even before the plans for a movie adaptation were announced. "*The Color Purple* was a seminal moment in my life. I read the book when it came out," she said in an interview. Oprah said she read the book and finished it in just one day, then went back to the book store the following day and bought every single copy they had available. She then passed out the copies to friends and co-workers in her office.

When plans for a film adaptation of *The Color Purple* surfaced, Oprah confessed she prayed hard to somehow end up in the movie. "And I say, 'God, you've got to get me in that movie. Now, I had never been in a movie. I didn't know anything about movies. But, I started praying to be in the movie. I was going to try to get in that movie," Oprah recalls. Quincy Jones, a producer who was affiliated with the production, saw Oprah on *AM Chicago* from his hotel room TV and immediately thought Oprah would be great for the role of Sofia, a housewife in the story.

Jones got his casting agent to contact Oprah, but they did not immediately reveal to her that it was for *The Color Purple*, keeping the project a secret by calling it *Moon Song*. Oprah was contacted to audition for *Moon Song*, to which she agreed, only to find out when she got to the audition and read the script that it was, indeed, for *The Color Purple*.

Oprah remarked, "I knew the whole book, so when I got to the audition and I read the sides, I was like, 'This is *The Color Purple*!'. It is amazing that I attracted this into my life. It was a miracle." She did not hear back for two months after the audition, so she called Reuben Cannon, the casting director, to ask why she has not heard back from them. Oprah says

Cannon's response was to ask her why she was calling him instead of them calling her, sternly reminding her that there are real actresses who auditioned for the same role. This included Alfre Woodard.

Dejected, Oprah hung up, thinking she would never get the part because she was up against Woodard. A short while later however, she got a call from Steven Spielberg himself, and found out that she got the part. Oprah says, "*The Color Purple* changed my life. It changed everything about my life because, in that moment of praying and letting go, I really understood the principle of surrender."

To be able to do the film, however, Oprah had to commit at least two months for filming. This conflicted with her schedule on *AM Chicago*, where she was doing about 220 shows each year and only had two weeks of vacation time. She begged her bosses at the TV station to give her an additional two weeks of vacation time so she could film, telling them she would not take a vacation for the next five years if only they let her take the time off for filming.

The bargaining paid off. *The Color Purple* debuted to overwhelmingly positive reviews from film critics, with accolades for the film's direction, acting ensemble, screenplay, musical scoring, and production values. Film critic Roger Ebert of the *Chicago Sun-Times* named it the best film of the year, heaping praise on newcomer Whoopi Goldberg as well. The movie was a box office success, earning over $142 million all over the world and screening in the United States for 21 weeks. It was 1985's top-grossing PG-13 film. The movie also garnered various nominations, including Oscar nominations for Best Picture, Best Actress, and Best Supporting Actress for Margaret Avery as well as for Oprah. Oprah was also nominated for a Golden Globe for Best Supporting Actress for her role in the film.

Oprah goes into national syndication

After *The Color Purple*, Oprah's popularity began to spread. The syndication offer from distributor King World was sealed, bringing *The Oprah Winfrey Show* to 138 American cities, a syndication record at the time. Her talk show won the time slot against *Donahue*, despite *Donahue* airing on more than two hundred TV stations. Oprah's show won the top ten United States TV markets, beating *Donahue* ratings by 31 percent. Interestingly, it was Donahue's style of having a more intimate conversation with his studio audience that Oprah also used, albeit with a more female emphasis. Oprah took the microphone with her to move through the audience, get a feel of their opinions and insights, and engaging in spirited and honest discussions. It resonated with the mostly female daytime audience, but also successfully crossed genders, ethnicities, age brackets, and other demographics. Topics on *The Oprah Winfrey Show* primarily discussed women's issues and affairs, but soon also delved into controversial issues of national importance and topics that other talk shows steered clear from.

The intense competition between *The Oprah Winfrey Show* and *Donahue* was the subject of much media fodder, especially as Oprah's show soon overtook Donahue in the ratings. An article for *TIME Magazine* noted that Oprah made up for her lack of 'journalistic toughness' by showing a lively mix of humor, curiosity, and empathy in speaking to her guests and audience members. "It is the talk show that is a group therapy session," stated to the magazine.

While the show was seen more as a tabloid talk show in its early seasons, the topics became more serious in the early to mid-1990's. Oprah shifted to more discussions on health and wellness, political discourse, spirituality, meditation, international social causes, and other news-related talk points. The show did still have its share of celebrity interviews and popular televised promotions and giveaways though.

One of the most notable television interviews Oprah hosted was a special primetime interview with Michael Jackson which aired in 1993. The 90-minute interview, which was

21

broadcast on ABC, was the top-rated show the week it aired. It still ranks as the fourth most-watched entertainment television program in history, averaging about 36.5 million viewers.

Oprah tries film acting again

The Color Purple would not be Oprah's only venture into acting. In 1998, she produced and starred in another film adaptation of a Pulitzer Prize-winning novel, this time Toni Morrison's *Beloved*. The story revolves around the character of Sethe, a former slave after the American Civil War. Oprah played the main character, and Danny Glover and Thandie Newton co-starred. The film was a box-office failure, only earning $23 million against a production budget of $80 million. Oprah famously said that after *Beloved* bombed at the box office and was beaten by the horror movie *Bride of Chucky*, she ate 30 pounds of macaroni and cheese. She has also publicly stated that *Beloved*'s box office disappointment was one of the lowest points of her career, and was one of the causes for her bout of major depression.

However, *Beloved* was widely praised by critics, and garnered an Oscar nomination for Best Costume Design (Colleen Atwood). To prepare for her role, Oprah agreed to undergo a 24-hour simulation of slavery, which entailed being tied up, blindfolded, and left by herself in the woods. Newton, her costar, described Oprah as very smart, acute, and a "strong technical actress" with a sharp mind.

Oprah has also lent her voice to several animated movies, including 2006's *Charlotte's Web*, 2007's *Bee Movie*, and 2009's *The Princess and the Frog*. She narrated the nature program *Life* for Discovery Networks, which was the US version of the BBC's original production.

Harpo Productions

The Winfrey touch in mass media extends to other television productions via her outfit, Harpo Productions. Founded in 1986 in Chicago, the multimedia production outfit is the subsidiary of Oprah's media and entertainment company, Harpo Inc. It has a little over 12,000 employees. Harpo Productions produced *The Oprah Winfrey Show* from 1986 until it aired its final episode in 2011.

Another famous production of Harpo is the daytime show *Dr. Phil*, hosted by Phil McGraw. McGraw was a frequent segment guest on *The Oprah Winfrey Show*, banking on his many experiences as a clinical and forensic psychologist to give advice and advocate life strategies to guests. *Dr. Phil* was co-produced by Harpo Productions until 2010.

Also a notable Harpo TV show is *The Dr. Oz Show*, which was co-produced with Sony Pictures. It features Mehmet Cengiz

Oz, a Turkish-American surgeon, Columbia University professor, and author who had appeared in many guest appearances on *The Oprah Winfrey Show*. Dr. Oz became popular as a proponent of alternative medicine. *The Dr. Oz Show* was launched in 2010, and the daily medical TV program continues in wide syndication until today.

Another frequent guest on *The Oprah Winfrey Show*, Nate Berkus, became very popular after his appearances on the show which led to another Harpo-produced broadcast syndicated show, *The Nate Berkus Show*. It featured mostly segments on interior design, home decor, culture, make-overs, lifestyle issues, and advice on other matters. Berkus was first featured on Oprah's talk show in 2005 when he recounted the loss of his partner, popular photographer Fernando Bengoechea, whom he was vacationing with in a Sri Lanka beach resort during the 2004 Indian Ocean tsunami.

Other Harpo Productions syndicated TV shows include: *Rachael Ray, The Rosie Show, Super Soul Sunday, Iyanla: Fix My Life, Oprah Prime, Oprah: Where Are They Now?, Oprah's Master Class*, and *Oprah's Lifeclass*.

Aside from Oprah's acting ventures, she has also ventured into the development and production of long-form television specials, films, and features through Harpo Films, which was the largest division under Harpo Productions until it was dissolved. Harpo Films was established in 1993 and supplied many award-winning features, such as the Oprah Winfrey Presents telefilms (or television movies) which aired on the ABC network. Harpo Films also entered a development and production deal with HBO in 2008.

Some feature films which were Harpo Films projects include *The Great Debaters, The Hundred Foot Journey, Selma,* and *Precious: Based on the Novel Push by Sapphire. Precious* was a co-production with Lee Daniels Entertainment, Smokewood Entertainment, and 34th Street Films, and garnered six Oscar nominations, including for Best Picture. Selma, starring David Oyelowo, Tom Wilkinson, Tim Roth, Carmen Ejogo, and Common, was nominated for multiple Golden Globe and Oscar nominations, and won Best Original Song at the 87th Oscars.

Television movies which were produced by Harpo Films include *Tuesdays with Morrie, The Wedding, Amy and Isabelle, Their Eyes Were Watching God, David and Lisa,* and *Oprah Winfrey Presents: Mitch Albom's For One More Day.*

Oprah writes, too

Oprah has also tried her hand at writing and publication. In 2005, she co-authored a book on weight loss together with her personal trainer Bob Greene. Entitled *The Best Life Diet*, it was disclosed that the advance fee that Oprah received for the book eclipsed the record previously set by former President Bill Clinton, who was paid an advance fee of $12 million. Other books that Oprah has authored or co-authored include *What I Know For Sure* (a collection of thoughts and quotes from the television host), *Food, Health and Happiness: 115 On-Point Recipes for Great Meals and a Better Life, Make The Connection: 10 Steps to a Better Body and a Better Life* (co-authored with Bob Greene), *The Wisdom of Sundays: Life-Changing Insights from Super Soul Conversations, The Best of Oprah's What I Know For Sure, Journey to Beloved,* and other collections, journals, and compilations.

In supermarket shelves and bookstores all over the world, you will see Oprah's face in her own magazine publication, *O, The Oprah Magazine.* It has been dubbed by *Fortune* Magazine as the most successful publishing start-up ever. The monthly publication first came out on April 19, 2000. By June of 2004, it was averaging 2.7 million paid circulation copies, two-thirds of which were subscriptions. In 2009, with the majority of US magazines experiencing declines in sales as a result of the recession, as well as the shift to online readership, *O, The Oprah Magazine* upped its newsstand sales by 5.8 percent. In 2004, Oprah also published the *O at Home* magazine, which ran for four years.

The *O Magazine* is known for having featured Oprah on the cover of every issue, with notable exceptions being shared covers with former First Lady Michelle Obama (April 2009) and Ellen DeGeneres (December 2009). Aside from the printed edition, *O Magazine* is also available digitally via the magazine's iPad app, which allows users to subscribe monthly or yearly, and features exclusive video content and previews of books featured in the magazine.

Oprah's online presence

With the shift to digital affecting media platforms, Oprah has also successfully made use of the internet as both a primary and complementary channel for her many media ventures. Her official website, Oprah.com, features a wide range of resources and content that supplements her TV show, network, productions, book club, charitable causes, and other activities. The website has an average of 70 million views each month, and about six million users monthly.

Notably, one of the most widely-publicized campaigns of Oprah.com was the "Oprah's Child Predator Watch List". Using her television show and the website, the campaign sought to help in capturing known fugitives wanted for various sex offenses against minors. The watch list showed the faces of fugitives being hunted by law enforcement, and within the first 48 hours after the list was published online, two of the wanted men were apprehended.

Oprah on satellite radio

Even radio has not escaped the Oprah presence, particularly satellite radio. In February of 2006, Oprah inked a three-year, $55 million deal with XM Satellite Radio, launching her very own satellite radio channel called Oprah Radio. The channel features shows and segments from popular contributors and guests on *The Oprah Winfrey Show*, many of whom have already started their own syndicated television programs. Oprah Radio has programs featuring trainer Bob Greene, Dr. Mehmet Oz, Nate Berkus, Marianne Williamson, Dr. Robin Smith, Dr. Maya Angelou, Gayle King, Rabbi Shumley Boteach, and more.

OWN launches

Of her various multimedia ventures, however, Oprah's biggest and most daring undertaking has been the Oprah Winfrey Network or OWN. The television channel, owned by Harpo Studios and Discovery Communications, was launched in January 2011, replacing the Discovery Health Channel and available to about 80 million U.S. households.

The Oprah Winfrey Network's programming relies heavily on

marathon daytime blocks featuring shows produced by Harpo Productions and other co-producers. Talk shows such as *Dr. Phil, The Nate Berkus Show* and *Rachael Ray* dominate OWN's primetime line-up, along with documentaries, TV specials, and movies. Original shows include *The Gayle King Show, Our America with Lisa Ling*, and *In The Bedroom with Dr. Laura Berman.*

OWN struck ratings gold when it entered into a partnership with popular comedian Tyler Perry in 2012. The deal guaranteed for all of Perry's original new television programs to be aired exclusively on OWN. The contract included 90 episodes of original content encompassing a Perry-produced drama (*The Haves and the Have Nots*), a comedy series *Love Thy Neighbor*, and the new season of *Tyler Perry's For Better or Worse*, which was carried over from TBS. *The Haves and the Have Nots* has been hailed as OWN's biggest ratings success story so far. Shows produced by Perry which air on OWN consistently garner at least one million viewers per episode.

Oprah's Book Club

Oprah also turned her love for reading books into a campaign to get her viewers and followers to read more. Ever since childhood, Oprah was already a voracious book reader, and this hobby aided in renewing her perspective on life and turning things around despite the challenges of her childhood. She particularly credits Dr. Maya Angelou's *I Know Why the Caged Bird Sings* for transforming her teenage years.

In her talk show, Oprah started a segment called Oprah's Book Club in 1996, where she featured and discussed books, mostly fiction, with a new recommendation every month. Over its 15-year-run, Oprah's Book Club featured 70 books, many of which were little known titles from obscure authors. An inclusion into Oprah's Book Club became a sure-fire way for a book to become a bestseller, with sales going up to several million copies for titles featured each month.

When *The Oprah Winfrey Show* aired its last episode on May 25, 2011, Oprah's Book Club also ceased to exist. But over a year later, Oprah launched Oprah's Book Club 2.0 as a joint campaign of OWN and *O, The Oprah Winfrey Magazine*, with the campaign encompassing different social networking sites and digital readers. The first title featured on Oprah's Book Club 2.0 was *Wild* by the author Cheryl Strayed.

Art and storytelling

Oprah was once asked why she was interested in combining all types of media platforms and entertainment in her career, to which she answered, "I see all art as a complement to telling people's stories. I'm in the storytelling business. I believe that the humanity that all of us share is the stories of our lives, and everybody has a story."

Oprah went on to say that she had a very important realization while looking back at her childhood and discovering that, even at a young age, her purpose in life was to highlight human stories, inspire and encourage others, and allow people to see their inner potential. "All those years, that's what I was trying to do, through my work and through the books that I highlighted."

Indeed, Oprah has come a long way from her roots in dirt-poor rural Mississippi to now becoming a wealthy multimedia force, and she is using her own experiences and struggles to inspire millions who look up to her for guidance and motivation.

Chapter Summary

- Oprah Winfrey was a fast-rising television personality in Chicago in the early 1980's, but her role in the Steven Spielberg period drama *The Color Purple* catapulted her to national prominence. Soon after, her talk show was syndicated nationally.
- Oprah had to bargain with her bosses on AM Chicago to allow her to take some time off so she could finish filming *The Color Purple*, which was one of her favorite books.
- The Oprah Winfrey Show was first distributed nationally by King World, airing on 138 television stations. It soon overtook erstwhile daytime talk show leader Donahue.
- Oprah's talk show started out as a tabloid talk show but evolved into a more serious daytime discussion on more political, social, spiritual, and health issues.
- Oprah's second film, *Beloved*, was praised by critics but a dismal box office failure. She admitted going into a state of depression after *Beloved* tanked.
- Oprah's Harpo Productions is the outfit that launched many popular nationally syndicated programs, featuring guests who started out as regular segment guests on her own talk show.
- In the world of publication, Oprah has authored and co-authored several books, and is also the face and subject of *O, The Oprah Magazine*.

- In 2011, Oprah started her own television channel, OWN. After a rocky start, OWN hit ratings success when it acquired original programming from entertainer Tyler Perry.
- Oprah's Book Club 2.0, a sequel to the popular Oprah's Book Club which ran for 15 years, continues to feature various authors and book titles recommended by Oprah herself.

Chapter Four: The Other Side of Oprah

"I am here to try to let people see through stories, to let people see the connection we have as human beings and how you can reach for the greatest for yourself. I mean, my life is an example of that." - Oprah Winfrey

---

Someone as immensely successful and popular as Oprah Winfrey may seem to many like an invincible force of nature bereft of the problems and challenges of normal people. As Oprah herself has revealed time and again to her audience, her life has been anything but smooth sailing. She has not been spared from experiencing her own share of failures, misfortunes, and missteps along the way. What is different with the Queen of All Media is how she has repeatedly used these obstacles to come out a better, stronger, more mature individual.

Battle against child abuse

As already discussed in a previous chapter, Oprah's childhood was difficult. The media personality was widely praised when she spoke about the molestation she suffered at the hands of her own family members at the age of nine, and she used this to shed light on a problem that many in America are hesitant to talk about publicly. At a gathering of thousands of college students at Indiana's Ball State University, she acknowledged that any person who has experienced some form of abuse, whether verbal or physical, "...will spend a great deal of their life rebuilding their esteem."

Drawing from her own experience as a survivor of child sexual abuse, Oprah became an outspoken advocate for social change in this regard, including publicly supporting the National Child Protection Act in the early 1990's. During that time, Oprah testified in front of the United States Senate judiciary committee about the need to set up a national database listing convicted child abuse offenders. Within a couple of years, then President Bill Clinton would sign the bill, known as the "Oprah Bill", into law.

Oprah's failed romantic relationships

Oprah has interviewed many famous personalities and celebrities regarding personal matters, but what is remarkable about her is she has never shied away from talking about her own life struggles as well, particularly her relationships. Oprah has never been married, but she did have several romantic relationships, such as high school sweetheart Anthony Otey (with whom she had talked about marriage but ended up breaking up with him in her senior year), college boyfriend William Taylor (who was not ready to move to Baltimore with her when she was offered a job at WJZ-TV), popular American composer and pianist John Frank Tesh, and fellow WJZ-TV reporter Lloyd Kramer.

In a magazine interview, Oprah also spoke about an intense love affair she experienced with a married man which lasted for four years. The man, however, had no plans of leaving his wife for Oprah, and this sent her into an emotional tailspin, with several episodes of desperate begging. At one point, she recalled contemplating suicide because of the failed love affair, even writing a suicide note to her best friend Gayle King.

Oprah points to these emotionally difficult relationships as triggers for her struggle with weight loss -- a battle which she has also openly shared with viewers, readers, and followers. She admits to wanting the approval of men so much but somehow always ending up in abusive relationships, or becoming too attached to men who were just self-absorbed and cared little for her. "The reason I gained so much weight in the first place and the reason I had such a sorry history of abusive relationships with men was I just needed approval so much. I needed everyone to like me, because I didn't like myself much," Oprah revealed.

Oprah has also talked about at least two romantic affairs she had that involved illegal drugs, including crack cocaine. On her talk show, Oprah recalled how she became addicted to the man, and started smoking crack cocaine because he was also using. Another former boyfriend of hers, Randolph Cook, claimed that he and Oprah lived together for a few months in the mid-1980s and they would do drugs together.

Oprah eventually finds love

Oprah had several other failed relationships, including a brief affair with film critic Roger Ebert, and a relationship with Haitian film director Reginald Chevalier. Soon, however, Oprah would meet Stedman Graham, with whom she has been with since 1986.

Oprah and Graham were engaged to be married sometime in 1992, but for some reason, the wedding ceremony never pushed through and is still in limbo until this day, although they are still a couple. In a 2003 interview with *Essence Magazine*, Oprah described theirs as the furthest thing from a 'traditional relationship'. "The truth of the matter is, had we gotten married we wouldn't be together now," she told the publication.

Her best friend, Gayle

A steady fixture in Oprah's colorful life is her closest friend Gayle King. The two have been inseparable since their early twenties, and Gayle has also gone on to host her own show on OWN, *The Gayle King Show*. When Gayle inked a co-anchor deal with *CBS This Morning*, her talk show ended on November 2011. Oprah and Gayle's very close friendship has been the subject of persistent gay rumors, which both have shrugged off. Addressing the rumors in an August 2006 issue of her magazine, Oprah said, "There isn't a definition in our culture for this kind of bond between women."

Other close friends of Oprah include Dr. Maya Angelou, trainer Bob Greene, designer Nate Berkus, Maria Shriver, Sidney Poitier, Denzel Washington, John Travolta, Julia Roberts, Halle Berry, and Forest Whitaker.

Anti-hip hop bias?

Despite her status as a celebrated talk show host, Oprah has also been involved in several controversies, particularly in 2006 when she was accused by popular rap music artists Ludacris, Ice Cube, and 50 Cent of being biased against hip-hop music. Ludacris alleged in a magazine interview that Oprah did not like many of his lyrics, and initially did not want to invite him with the rest of the cast of the movie *Crash* when they appeared on her show.

50 Cent made a similar complaint, saying, "I think she caters to older white women." Ice Cube, meanwhile, told *FHM* that Oprah invited Cedric the Entertainer and Eve to appear on her show to promote the film *Barbershop*, but left him out. "Maybe she's got a problem with hip-hop," according to Ice Cube.

Oprah responded to the controversy by saying that while she does enjoy the music of many artists in the urban and hip-hop genre, she personally opposes rap lyrics that marginalize females. Oprah also explained that she had talked to Ludacris personally regarding this and aired her side, and commented that while she understood that his music and lyrics are meant for entertainment, there are listeners who may also be taking the messages literally.

The politics of Oprah under scrutiny

Her perceived political biases have also been occasionally

39

targeted, particularly during the 2008 election campaign when Matt Drudge of the *Drudge Report* said she did not allow Sarah Palin to guest on her show. At the time, Oprah was outspoken in her support of Barack Obama for president. It was alleged that Oprah purposely did not want to book Palin as a guest because she was supporting the Democratic ticket, an allegation that Oprah denied.

"There has been absolutely no discussion about having Sarah Palin on my show," Oprah's statement said. "I agree that Sarah Palin would be a fantastic interview, and I would love to have her on after the campaign is over." Palin did go on Oprah's show on November 18, 2009, after the election season.

The James Frey scandal

Another controversy Oprah had to weather was the fallout from the inclusion of disgraced author James Frey's memoir, *A Million Little Pieces*. Frey, who founded the media production company Full Fathom Five, wrote the purported memoir in 2003, but it was later discovered that large sections of the story were either grossly exaggerated or completely fabricated. Oprah invited Frey and his publisher Nan Talese to her show for a live interview on January 26, 2006, in which she confronted their claims.

Weight loss battles

Despite the different obstacles she has had to face, Oprah has shown remarkable resolve and resilience, especially under intense scrutiny and media attention. This has been exemplified perhaps most notably in her very public weight loss struggles which she has continued to share with her audience.

In the 1980s, at the start of her talk show career, Oprah already tackled her weight loss journey, famously pulling a wagon with 67 pounds of fat behind her on an episode of The Oprah Winfrey Show in 1988, to highlight her very much slimmer figure in tight jeans and a black turtleneck sweater. The episode, entitled "Diet Dreams Come True", enjoined her daytime audience to her weight loss goals and resonated with much of her audience also going through the same struggle. Oprah would go on to co-author several books with her personal trainer Bob Greene, highlighting the many realizations she had to face about her body's physical needs, the difficulties of maintaining the weight she wanted, and her bouts of discontent. Even her investment into Weight Watchers stock became part of the diet conversation.

These days, Oprah's public discussions regarding weight have evolved from maintaining a 'slim figure' to simply finding the right shape that you are comfortable in, and focusing on becoming a healthier version of yourself while not giving in to society's perception of what is too big or too small. Still, it cannot be denied that her very public and frank discussions regarding weight loss, whether on her television show, social media platforms, books, magazines, or media interviews, have made it a more honest discourse for society in general, as she allowed the public to see a side of her which many famous celebrities would rather keep private.

Chapter Summary

- Oprah Winfrey has endeared herself even more to her audience because of her openness to discussing her own life experiences, whether good or bad.
- She used her own ordeal as a survivor of childhood sexual abuse to convince U.S. lawmakers to sign into law a national database for sex offenders.
- Oprah's many romantic encounters have mirrored her desire to be loved and accepted, often leading to abusive relationships.
- Oprah's boyfriend since 1986, Stedman Graham, is still her partner to this day. They have remained unmarried.
- Gayle King, Oprah's best friend since the 1970's, has also become a media personality of her own.
- Several controversies have hounded Oprah's career in the past, including perceived biases against rap music artists. She was also alleged to have banned Sarah Palin from appearing on her show during the 2008 election campaign, which she denied.
- Oprah's very public struggles with weight loss have triggered national conversations about healthy living and a redefinition of what is more important as far as fitness and wellness.

Chapter Five: A Greater Purpose

"Making other people happy is what brings me happiness." – Oprah Winfrey

---

To say that Oprah has achieved success would be a bit of an understatement. Her influence in the United States and around the world has been underscored time and again by numerous publications and media entities. Both CNN and *Time* magazine have hailed Oprah as "arguably the most influential woman in the world", while Life noted that she is the most influential black person of her generation. *Forbes* Magazine dubbed Oprah the most powerful celebrity in the world five different years (2005, 2007, 2008, 2010, 2013). Her influence on society, particularly on media matters, political discourse, television talk shows, and perceptions of beauty and size have been discussed in detail, with *The Wall Street Journal* even referring to her style of public confession as 'Oprah-fication'. Regarding her interview style, *Time*

Magazine came up with the moniker 'rapport talk', saying Oprah's talent lies in the seamless conglomeration of public and private matters, making television and communication a more intimate duopoly. "She makes people care because she cares. That is Winfrey's genius, and will be her legacy, as the changes she has wrought in the talk show continue to permeate our culture and shape our lives," a 1998 *Time* article declared.

Changing mainstream acceptance

Oprah has also been viewed as one of the trailblazers of a new brand of tabloid talk show that has paved the way for a more open and understanding perception of the lesbian, gay, bisexual, and transgender (LGBT) community. Although *Donahue* came first, Oprah made the tabloid talk show more relatable to a wider mainstream audience because of her intimate and personal style. As Oprah's talk show found greater success, more tabloid talk shows such as *The Jenny Jones Show, Ricki Lake, Geraldo*, and *Jerry Springer* followed suit, all focusing on topics that were previously taboo or viewed as outside mainstream media, including LGBT issues.

Oprah's effect on politics

Even in the political scene, it cannot be denied that Oprah has a profound impact. During the 2008 presidential campaign, Oprah threw her support behind Democratic candidate Barack Obama. It would be the first time that she would publicly endorse any political candidate. When asked by CNN's Larry King why she decided to publicly endorse Obama, Oprah answered, "I think that what he stands for, what he has proven that he can stand for, what he has shown was worth me going out on a limb for – and I haven't done it in the past because I haven't felt that anybody, I didn't know anybody well enough to be able to say, I believe in this person."

In the same interview, Oprah also mentioned that while she endorsed Obama publicly, she has not made a financial contribution to his campaign, realizing that there is a limit to how much financial donations he can accept. She said that her value to Obama's presidential run is the weight and influence of her support, and this would be worth much more than writing a check.

In many ways, this turned out to be an accurate assessment, particularly as Oprah accompanied Obama in a number of political rallies across important states such as South Carolina, New Hampshire, and Iowa. On December 9, 2007, an Obama rally featuring Oprah which was held at the William Bryce Football Stadium in Columbia, South Carolina saw over 30,000 people attending.

During the rally, Oprah harked back to a famous African-American leader who, just a few decades prior to that moment, envisioned a better America for all races. "I've been inspired to believe that a new vision is possible for America. Dr. King dreamed the dream. But we don't have to just dream the dream anymore. We get to vote that dream into reality," Oprah told the cheering crowd.

A study by two economists out of the University of Maryland, College Park estimated that Oprah's endorsement delivered up to 1.6 million votes for Obama during the Democratic primary, translating to the gap in the popular vote between Obama and his closest rival Hillary Clinton.

Oprah's role as spiritual adviser

Oprah's role in the evolving sense of spirituality and philosophy of the modern generation has also been discussed in detail. A 2002 article which appeared on *Christianity Today* dubbed Oprah as a spiritual leader with immense influence, calling her empire "The Church of O". "To her audience of more than 22 million mostly female viewers, she has become a postmodern priestess — an icon of church-free spirituality," Christianity Today said.

Several popular spiritual teachers have appeared on Oprah's talk show, including Gary Zukav, author of the book *The Seat of the Soul*. Zukav first appeared in 1998 on *The Oprah Winfrey Show* and guested 3 times, the most of any guest. Oprah gushed that Zukav's book *The Seat of the Soul* is her favorite book of all time aside from the Bible, and that she keeps a copy of it on her bedside. Another spiritual teacher who was publicly endorsed by Oprah was Eckhart Tolle, author of *A New Earth: Awakening to Your Life's Purpose*.

The ambiguous, homogeneous, and purposely New Age spirituality and thinking of Oprah has not come without its many critics. While she was raised a Baptist, Oprah has publicly stated that she does not believe Christianity is the only path to God. In response, *Crosswalk.com* commentator and radio talk show host Frank Pastore pointed out that her New Age beliefs are not in line with traditional Christianity. "If she's a Christian, she's an ignorant one, because Christianity is incompatible with New Age thought," Pastore wrote.

Bill Keller, founder of the web-based faith program *LivePrayer.com*, even went so far as saying Oprah is appealing to a large number of people akin to a drug. "She has an incredible amount of influence over people and an incredible following. I believe these New Age teachings are like 'spiritual crack' because people are hungry, the teachings satisfy and then they are hungry again," Keller said.

Oprah the philanthropist

What should be apparent to all, whether a fan or a critic, is how she has used her following to impact positive change in the United States and around the world. Oprah became the first African-American philanthropist to enter the Top 50 list of BusinessWeek, which lists the biggest charitable givers in the U.S.

Oprah is a firm believer in giving to educational causes, and she has contributed upwards of $400 million towards various educational causes across the world. One such campaign she supported is Christmas Kindness South Africa, launched in 2002, which gave food, shoes, clothes, school supplies, books, and toys to over 50,000 children from rural schools and orphanages in South Africa.

Oprah's foundation, according to her, exists to provide educational opportunities for the less fortunate around the world, highlighting her belief that a better education leads to more freedom. "My foundation will continue to focus primarily on funding education projects globally. I believe that education is freedom. It provides the tools to affect one's own destiny. My gifts are more focused and directed toward making immediate change," she said.

The Oprah Winfrey Foundation has been responsible for

starting various initiatives throughout the world, focusing on women and children in low-income areas. Charitable organizations and causes that meet the Foundation's criteria for women and children empowerment are eligible to receive grants from the Foundation, and many such organizations have been financially assisted by the Oprah Winfrey Foundation to provide school supplies, finance school buildings and facilities, and provide scholarships to children all over the world.

Oprah is passionate about using her special position in society to become a blessing to those she can help. "I have a blessed life, and I have always shared my life's gifts with others ... I will continue to use my voice and my life as a catalyst for change, inspiring and encouraging people to help make a difference in the lives of others. I'm fortunate that the work I do in my life becomes more meaningful with every experience," she has stated. declara, afirma

Another large charity started by Oprah which has been instrumental in various causes worldwide is Oprah's Angel Network, which was launched in 1998 and works with various projects and non-profit organizations. Oprah personally supported the administrative costs of Angel Network, meaning 100% of the donations sent to the charity were channeled to different programs.

Oprah's Angel Network was able to raise over $80 million dollars for various causes, including a $1 million contribution from singer Jon Bon Jovi. One of the charity's most significant projects was the Oprah Angel Network Katrina registry which was launched after Hurricane Katrina devastated much of the Gulf Coast. Oprah herself personally donated $10 million to assist victims of Hurricane Katrina as well as to rebuild destroyed communities.

When *The Oprah Winfrey Show* ended, Oprah's Angel Network also ceased from accepting monetary donations, but Oprah continues to support a number of philanthropic and charitable organizations to this day. She has also once said that because she does not have any maternal children of her own, she feels a connection to the girls she supports at the Oprah Winfrey Leadership Academy for Girls in South Africa. "I want to have a presence they can sense and feel comfortable with," she noted.

Oprah also sees comparisons between her humble beginnings and the backgrounds of many of the South African girls who attend the school. "I see myself in all these girls--the struggles and the hardships that just seem unbearable. I have nothing but respect for them," Oprah said.

The remarkable life that Oprah has lived has undoubtedly made her the unique multimedia personality that she is today, and it is fascinating to appreciate how she has taken the lessons she learned from childhood and all throughout her career to become a catalyst for change and charity. In a society where many are focused on amassing wealth and getting ahead of everyone else, Oprah is a constant reminder of the importance to empower others to leave a legacy of generosity and kindness.

Chapter Summary

- Oprah Winfrey is one of the most influential voices of today, and is ranked among the wealthiest, but is also one of the biggest philanthropic givers.
- The influence of Oprah on society has been dubbed the "Oprah-fication" of society by The Wall Street Journal.
- Oprah has been credited for the more mainstream acceptance of the LGBT community.
- Sociologists also point to The Oprah Winfrey Show as the precursor for the new brand of tabloid talk shows permeating daytime TV today.
- In the 2008 presidential campaign, Oprah publicly endorsed Barack Obama, the first time she ever endorsed a political candidate.
- Oprah is credited for delivering more than a million votes for Obama.
- The spirituality of Oprah has often been described as a church of its own, drawing both praise and criticism from observers.
- The Oprah Winfrey Foundation supports a number of initiatives in the United States and around the world, focusing on educational causes for children in low-income communities.
- Oprah believes that a better education is a key to a better life and more freedom for the individual.
- Oprah also supports the Oprah Winfrey Leadership Academy for Girls in South Africa.

Chapter Six: What's Next?

"I have learned that being-fully-present thing. I am 1,000 percent fully present."
– Oprah Winfrey

Although *The Oprah Winfrey Show* officially ended its broadcast run in 2011, Oprah has been anything but absent from the public eye. The Queen of All Media continues to be an active contributor across media platforms, and is slated to join the popular CBS Sunday evening news program *60 Minutes*. Oprah has said that her decision to join *60 Minutes* is spurred on by a desire to help unite America.

"At a time when people are so divided, my intention is to bring relevant insight and perspective, to look at what separates us, and help facilitate real conversations between people from different backgrounds," Oprah said when asked about the *60 Minutes* gig.

Oprah starred in an HBO movie in 2017 called *The Immortal Life of Henrietta Lacks*, where she played the role of a cervical cancer patient diagnosed in the 1950's. Oprah also co-produced the HBO movie together with Alan Ball and Lydia Dean Pilcher. Oprah is also lending her voice to an animated comedy called *The Star*, revolving around a group of animals involved in the first Christmas. Oprah will be voicing a camel named Deborah.

There are two starring roles for Oprah coming in 2018: *Terms of Endearment*, which is a remake of a film from 1983, and *A Wrinkle in Time*, where she co-stars with Chris Pine and Reese Witherspoon. Meanwhile, in the publication scene, Oprah's new cookbook *Food, Health, and Happiness* hits bookstores next year as well, and features recipes she has gleaned from many years of diet plans. What is apparent in the newer cookbooks and recipe collections from Oprah is the increased attention to a more inclusive idea of what is healthy and fit, rather than the focus on "slimming" and weight loss from years past.

President Oprah in 2020?

But what has sent many tongues wagging is a possible Oprah Winfrey presidential run in 2020. In a Bloomberg interview with David Rubenstein, when asked whether she would consider running against Donald Trump for the top post in the land, Oprah answered, "I thought 'Oh gee, I don't have the experience. I don't know enough.' And now I'm thinking... Oh!"

Trump versus Winfrey in 2020? Now that would be a television event you would not want to miss.

Chapter Summary

- Oprah Winfrey is still highly visible these days, even though her syndicated talk show ended six years ago.
- There are various film projects in the pipeline for Oprah, including a remake of *Terms of Endearment*. She also co-stars in *A Wrinkle in Time* with Reese Witherspoon and Chris Pine.
- The long-running CBS Sunday news program *60 Minutes* will feature Oprah as one of its contributors starting this year.
- There are speculations that Oprah may consider running for president in 2020, possibly setting up a showdown against current U.S. President Donald Trump.

Chapter Seven: Rules for Success

When Oprah Winfrey speaks, the world listens. Health – both emotional and physical, and general wellness are the topics she often focuses upon. She is completely transparent with her own struggles in these areas, allowing herself to be relatable whilst also inspiring change. Here are ten of the most important life lessons Oprah has constantly preached over the years. A woman certainly worth listening to.

Rule #1. Always make time for yourself

"I give myself a healthy dose of quiet time at least once (and when I'm on point, twice) a day,"

Oprah is a firm believer in the benefits of transcendental meditation. Meditation can promote a state of relaxed awareness and set you up to face the day in a cool, calm and collected manner. This is her healthy dose of quiet time that she gives to herself that we could all benefit from. Oprah practices meditation for 20 minutes in the morning and 20 minutes at night. A good starting point for anyone new to meditation are the apps "headspace" and "calm" which will guide you through the process.

Rule #2. Practice an attitude of gratitude

"Every morning when I open my curtains for that first look at the day, no matter what the day looks like – raining, foggy, overcast, sunny – my heart swells with gratitude. I get another chance." Make this a morning habit from the moment you open your eyes and your day will be exponentially better. Gratitude is like a seed you plant; it grows more as it is watered and nourished. Oprah doesn't believe in alarm clocks. Instead she prefers to put the number in her mind and will wake up before then. Her first thought? *"Oh, I'm alive. Thank you!"* Happiness begins within.

Rule #3. Stay present

"Breathe. Let go. And remind yourself that this very moment is the

only one you know you have for sure,"

Many times Oprah has stressed the importance of living in the moment. It is all we truly have. Life does not exist in future anxieties or past embarrassments, there is only the here and now. Cherish it.

Rule #4. Work on yourself

"The number one thing you have to do is to work on yourself and build yourself up and keep your cup full."

The moment we believe we have it all figured out is the moment things will start to go wrong. Keep up your personal growth, immerse yourself in learning, become a master of your craft. Through working on ourselves, we are eventually able to offer the world so much more.

Rule #5. Find balance

"I can eat anything I want; I just can't eat it at the same time... Which is the entire philosophy of life: You can have it all. You just can't have it all at the same time."

Life is all about balance. There needs to be time for work and play. Healthy food and comfort food. Exercise and relaxing. Get the balance right and your life will improve whilst also allowing time for your chosen pleasures.

Rule #6. Relax, it's going to be okay

"I know how scared you are. If I could say anything to you, it would be 'Relax, it's going to be OK'".

Everyone gets scared. Working on your dreams and life in general can get overwhelming. Taking the risks you know you need to take can be damn near terrifying. When times get tough, remind yourself that "this too shall pass". By relaxing into whatever struggles arise, we remain flexible and open to inspiration and insight. Whatever it is that you're going through likely won't be happening a year from now.

Rule #7. Everyone makes mistakes

"You don't have to hold yourself hostage to who you used to be or anything you ever used to do. Who has lived and hasn't made mistakes?"

Tying in nicely with the last point, mistakes are going to happen. Everybody makes mistakes, the key is to learn from them. Oprah has admitted she used to give power over to people who didn't mean well for her. She has learned that it is completely within her control to stop giving that power away. Each setback should only be viewed as a learning curve. Just focus on the next right move, and do that. When success is viewed as one step at a time, there's no such thing as failure.

Rule #8. Follow your own beauty standards

"Gone, for me, are the days of wanting to be thin to fit into anything other than my best body and best life,"

Live for yourself and not the opinions of others. After a very public life-long battle with her weight issues, Oprah has learned it's best to be comfortable in the skin she's in. She stresses the importance of not trying to look perfect, just aim for your best you.

Rule #9. Find your purpose and run the race as hard as you can!

"If you don't know your purpose, your immediate goal is to figure that out."

The moment you find your purpose everything will start to make sense. Figuring out your why will increase your desire, energy and overall drive. Basically everything will start to fit into place. The problem? Plenty of people don't yet know their purpose. This is something that doesn't usually come overnight and needs to be worked upon but a good starting point is to follow these five steps.

Step 1: Find out what drives you

Step 2: Find out what energizes you

Step 3: Find out what you are willing to sacrifice for.

Step 4: Find out who you want to help.

Step 5: Find out how you want to help.

Once you've figured out your purpose?

"You just need to run that race as hard as you can. You need to give it everything you've got, all the time, for yourself."

Rule #10. Realize deep down we're all the same

"Everybody wants to fulfil the highest, truest, expression of yourself as a human being."

Oprah believes there is no difference between you and her. At the very core, we all want the same thing. To fulfil the highest, truest, expression of ourselves as a human being. Some us do this through business, some through construction. There are a variety of means, but at the end of the day we are all seeking the same thing. Oprah also believes that there is no luck. To make the most of the opportunities we are all given it is about preparing yourself fully. If you're not prepared for the opportunity, you can't make the most of it. So prepare yourself and then seize the opportunities that come your way. There is no luck.

"Nothing about my life is lucky. Nothing. Luck is preparation meeting the moment of opportunity."

Chapter Eight: Little Known Facts

Below I have compiled forty interesting facts on the Queen of All Media. I'm sure you will know a few already but hopefully the majority are new to you.

Oprah Winfrey's family was so poor growing up that, as a child, Winfrey was teased at school for wearing dresses made of potato sacks.

Oprah is at least 8% Native American - something she discovered when undergoing a DNA test for the PBS show African American Lives.

Two days after starting kindergarten, she wrote to her teacher saying: "I don't think I belong here 'cause I know a lot of big words." The teacher agreed and she skipped to first grade.

Oprah was anchoring the news at Nashville's WTVF-TV when she was just 19, making her the youngest person and the first African-American woman to hold the position.

Winfrey has donated her voice for an array cartoon characters, voicing Gussie the goose for Charlotte's Web, and Eudora, the mother of Princess Tiana in Disney's The Princess and the

Frog, among others.

Oprah's interview with Michael Jackson became the 4th most watched event in American television history, as well as the most watched interview of all-time, with 36 million viewers. Winfrey is credited for popularizing the intimate, confessional form of talk show, which has since become common across cable networks.

She was instrumental in launching Oxygen Media, dedicated to producing cable programming specifically for women. Oprah is the first black woman billionaire and the current richest African-American woman.

She is also referred to by many as the most influential woman in the world.

In 2013, Winfrey was awarded the Presidential Medal of Freedom (the nation's highest civilian honor) by President Barack Obama.

Winfrey was fired from her first job as an anchor. Seven and a half months in, Winfrey was given the boot and reportedly told by a producer she was "unfit for television news." "I had no idea what I was in for or that this was going to be the greatest growing period of my adult life," Winfrey later said. "It shook me to my very core."

Winfrey has been engaged to Stedman Graham since 1992. As to why the couple has yet to tie the knot? Winfrey told a reporter in 2013: "If you ever interviewed [Graham], he would tell you that had we married, we would not be together today. Because he's a traditional man and this is a very untraditional relationship. And I think it's acceptable as a relationship, but if I had the title 'wife,' I think there would be other expectations for what a wife is and what a wife does."

She lives most of the time on "The Promised Land", her 42-acre estate with ocean and mountain views in Montecito, California. Oprah also owns homes in Lavallette, New Jersey; an apartment in Chicago; an estate on Fisher Island, Florida; a ski house in Telluride, Colorado; and property on Maui, Hawaii and Antigua.

The only way to get to Winfrey's home in Colorado is by gondola. The $14 million mansion is located in an area of Telluride called Mountain Village. To get there, you must take a 10-minute gondola ride up one side of a mountain and down the other.

In one of her early TV gigs, the news director of a Baltimore TV station proposed to change her name to Suzy.

Her director at the Baltimore TV station also sent her to New York for a makeover at a salon that gave her a French perm. Her hair fell out.

She was sent to a juvenile hall for wayward girls in her younger years, but was turned away because there weren't enough beds.

In order to get her mother to buy her a more fashionable pair of glasses, Oprah once faked a robbery when living in her Milwaukee home. Even going so far as to overturn furniture and breaking her glasses!

Growing up, to say that she wasn't too fond of her name is an understatement. She hated it with "actual passion."

Her natural-born leader personality has been evident since young. In High School she was elected President of Student Council, with the slogan, "Vote for the Grand Ole Oprah."

Oprah ran a marathon in 1994 with an official finishing time of 4:29:15.

When asked how she prepares for an interview, she said she never prepares questions. "I just kind of sit and have a conversation".

The Wall Street Journal coined the term "Oprahfication", meaning public confession as a form of therapy. By confessing intimate details about her weight problems, tumultuous love life, and sexual abuse, and crying alongside her guests, Time magazine credits Winfrey with creating a new form of media communication known as "rapport talk."

In 1983, she made a guest appearance on an episode of "All My Children."

Her legendary TV career has earned her 39 Emmys, on top of

Oscar and Golden Globe nominations for "The Color Purple" in 1985.

In 1998 she received the National Academy of Television Arts and Sciences' Lifetime Achievement Award after which she withdrew from future Emmy consideration.

The power of Oprah's opinions and endorsement to influence public opinion, especially consumer purchasing choices, has been dubbed "The Oprah Effect."

In her very first talk show, "People Are Talking" in 1978, she had as guest the owner of the local Carvel ice cream store.

The theme of her first nationally televised "Oprah Winfrey Show," on Sept. 8, 1986, was how to catch a man.

At the peak of its rating, during 1991 and 1992, "The Oprah Winfrey Show" amassed about 13 million viewers each night.

She has two cocker spaniels called Sophie and Solomon.

She was elected the 2008 Person of the Year by animal-rights group People for the Ethical Treatment of Animals (PETA) for using her fame and listening audience to help the less fortunate, including animals.

Every week, her email box gets flooded by around 12,000 e-mails from fans all over the world.

Oprah has a particular liking for cream-colored pashmina pajamas.

When it comes to food, to her, nothing beats a good spicy

chicken from the Chicken Shack in Nashville and mashed potatoes with horseradish.

In 1988, she underwent a liquid diet regime which allowed her to lose 67 pounds in just four months. However, she put on back the weight two years later.

Over several years, she sponsored about 100 black men through college with a $7 million in scholarships.

In one of her first jobs in 1976, she made $225 a week as a TV news reporter.

In 2004, she became the first black person to rank among the 50 most generous Americans and she remained among the top 50 until 2010. By 2012 she had given away about $400 million to educational cause.

Conclusion

She has been ranked the richest African American of the 20th century, the greatest black philanthropist in American history, and was once the world's only black billionaire.

Some, for good reason, even consider her to be the most influential woman in the world right now.

There can be no doubting the inspiration and influence she has had to women and men from around the globe. She overcame a terrible start in life to run the most successful talk show of all time for nearly three decades, not to mention her countless other achievements. The journey that is Oprah's life is about overcoming the odds and we would be fools not to learn the many lessons she has to offer. I will leave you with one final quote of hers from a commencement speech she gave:

"I leave this with everyone in the room, graduates, friends of graduates, family... Your legacy is every life you've touched. Your legacy is every life you've touched. Feel everything with love, because every moment you are building your legacy."

Long live the queen of all media.

Thanks for checking out my book. I hope you found this of value and enjoyed it. But before you go, I have one small favor to ask…

Would you take 60 seconds and write a quick blurb about this book on Amazon?

Reviews are the best way for independent authors (like me) to get noticed, sell more books, and it gives me the motivation to continue producing. I also read every review and use the feedback to write future revisions – and even future books.

Thanks again.

Printed in Great Britain
by Amazon